Little Gidding

Story & Guide

by

Robert Van de Weyer

LAMP

Lamp Press
Marshall Pickering
34–42 Cleveland Street, London, W1P 5FB UK

First published in 1989 by Marshall Morgan and Scott
Publications Ltd
Part of the Marshall Pickering Holdings Group

British Library Cataloguing in Publication Data
Weyer, Robert Van de
  Little Gidding: story and guide
  1. Cambridgeshire. Little Gidding.
  Religious communities. Community of
  Christ the Sower, history
  I. Title
  271'.009426'5

ISBN: 0–551–01826–7

Text Set in Baskerville by Input Typesetting Ltd,
London
Printed in Great Britain by Cox & Wyman Ltd,
Reading

Contents

Acknowledgement

Most of the illustrations are by Hamish Moyle. The picture of Little Gidding Community Courtyard and the Map are by Michael Tilley.

Preface

Little Gidding now attracts many thousands of visitors each year, mostly to visit the church used by Nicholas Ferrar and his community in the 17th century, but some also to gain an impression of the present community living there. Leighton Bromswold, where with the Ferrars' help the poet George Herbert restored the church, has also become increasingly popular, and the community at Little Gidding now has a branch there, based at the beautiful Jacobean manor house near the church. Both places, despite their popularity, remain quiet and remote, inviting the visitor simply to relax and be still.

This short book is for those who want to learn more about the original community of Nicholas Ferrar, and also the formative years of the present community. In addition it contains a guide for the visitor both to Little Gidding and to Leighton Bromswold. Now, as in the past, the community welcomes visitors. There is a 'parlour' at Little Gidding containing an exhibition of the community's history; and there is ample accommodation in the community guest house at Leighton Bromswold for those wishing to stay.

Our Founders

The Common Root

The common root of all Christian communities is the first church in Jerusalem, described in the New Testament. Here the Christians met each day for prayer and meditation, they shared meals regularly, and, most strikingly of all, they pooled their possessions.

From that spectacular beginning two distinct forms of Christian community life developed. The first, which embraced the majority of Christians, was that of the parish church, in which members came together each Sunday for worship, but otherwise lived in ordinary homes doing normal jobs. The second was that of the monastery: single men or women living in a residential community in which every aspect of daily life was subject to a common rule.

During the happier periods of the Church's history these two ways of life were seen as complementary: the monks and nuns embodied the prophetic vision of Christ, in which the whole of life is subject to God's kingship; while Christians living in villages and towns sought to interpret that vision in the practical affairs of the world. But frequently monasteries and parish churches were at odds: monks, especially in the earlier centuries, were often quick to condemn the compromises which ordinary Christians were forced to make; while the monks themselves were often regarded as escapists or parasites of society — criticisms which by the later medieval period were largely true.

Yet, although these two forms of Christian life remained for the most part quite separate, there were attempts to bridge the gulf. In the 12th century St Francis formed a Third Order, which was a loose-knit community of people living in the world, following a simple rule of life based on that of the Franciscan friars. The Protestant reformation was nurtured in radical communities in central Europe, in which families sought to copy the life of the first Christian church in Jerusalem. But it was in England that the most deliberate attempts were made to fuse the monastery and the parish. Thomas Cranmer, in composing the new English Prayer Book, took the old monastic daily office and compressed it into two services, Matins and Evensong, designed to be said in ordinary parish churches and family homes. Thus the life of shared prayer was no longer to be confined to monks and nuns, but was for every Christian.

It was this vision, embodied in the Prayer Book, that inspired two young men, Nicholas Ferrar and George Herbert, in the early 17th century. With his brother and sister, their respective families, and with his indomitable mother Mary, Nicholas Ferrar established a religious community in the old manor house at Little Gidding. Children and teenagers, as well as adults, shared in the daily prayer, processing each day to the church like monks to say Matins and Evensong. George Herbert, inspired by his friend Nicholas's example, sought to make his own parish church the centre of a praying community: he and his wife Jane, and their household, would walk across to the church each morning and afternoon, inviting others in the parish to join them.

After the death of their founding members these experiments in community died out, but their memory lingered in the imagination of English Christians. And in the 20th century, during which there has been a great renewal of interest in community life, many have looked back to Ferrar and Herbert as trail-blazers. Our community is part of this new movement. We are especially privileged because our mother house is at Little Gidding itself, and we have a branch at Leighton Bromswold, five miles away, which was George

Nicholas Ferrar

Herbert's first parish. In seeking to establish our own way of life, we have found ourselves constantly looking back to their example, and also beyond them to the monastic tradition. Whenever we have gone wrong, it is because we have failed to learn the lessons of the past; and when things go right, it is because we are firmly attached to our roots. In our rule of life — published under the title The Little Gidding Way — we deliberately recall the Rule of St Benedict, who was the founder of monastic life in the Western Church, and also the example of St Pachomius, who founded the original monasteries in the desert of Egypt; and of course we recall the example and teaching of the two men whom we regard as our founders: Nicholas Ferrar and George Herbert.

So it is with Nicholas Ferrar and George Herbert, and their early lives, that our story begins . . .

Nicholas Ferrar

Nicholas Ferrar was born in 1592, the third son of a wealthy business man who was one of the founders of the Virginia Company, set up to colonize the New World. Both father and mother were devoutly religious, and Nicholas himself was a serious-minded, rather priggish child, who preferred to stay indoors reading to playing outside with friends. His favourite book was Foxe's Book of Martyrs, which included an account of his ancestor, Bishop Ferrar of St David's, who was burnt at the stake in 1555 for his unbending Protestant opposition to Queen Mary. From the age of six Nicholas wanted to be a clergyman, and announced to his mother that, whatever his brothers wore, he would not wear lace, but only plain clothes as befitted a future priest. When he was confirmed by the Bishop of London in 1598 he managed to have hands laid on him twice, explaining proudly afterwards: 'I did it because it was a good thing to have the Bishop's prayers and blessings twice, and I have got it.'

Some time afterwards he had an experience which he came to regard as his true conversion to the Christian faith. It occurred one cold and frosty night, shortly before he was to be sent away to boarding school. He was unable to sleep, and as the night hours passed he was overcome by a sense of remorse. He got out of bed, went into the garden, and threw himself face downwards on the frozen grass, sobbing and crying. He begged God that 'true fear and care of his divine majesty' would fill his heart, and 'that this fear and love of God might never depart' from him; and he prayed that God would reveal 'how he must serve him'. Gradually he felt a great weight lifting from his heart, and at last he stood up and returned to bed, inwardly peaceful. The intensity of this childhood experience stayed with him for the rest of his life, and as an adult in his daily prayers he consciously renewed the commitment he made on that night.

At the age of 13 he was sent to Cambridge University, where he studied at Clare Hall under Austin Linsell, later Bishop of Peterborough. Nicholas was academically bright and his conversation was stimulating and witty, so that after a year he was elected a Fellow Commoner, sitting at high table amongst the Fellows. Linsell encouraged Nicholas to read the works of the early Fathers of the Church, and Nicholas, an impressionable teenager, tried to model his life on theirs: he ate sparingly; he rose early to go to prayers at five o'clock in the college chapel, and he read till late at night; he dressed simply, and scrupulously avoided the more bawdy student pastimes.

But throughout his time at Cambridge Nicholas suffered from what his physician described as 'aguish dispositions' which were attacks of high fever, sometimes with a rash breaking out on his body. The usual prescription was starvation which Nicholas, inspired by the saints, seems to have relished. But the attacks grew more severe and frequent, and eventually the doctor declared that it was the cold, damp climate of

Cambridge that was at fault. So, in 1613, Nicholas was forced to abandon a promising academic career, and to travel abroad in the hope that a warmer climate would restore his health. He expected to die during his journey, and wrote a long letter to his parents, which was filled with self-pity, and resentment at life's unfair treatment of him.

He spent three years touring Europe, and proved a most resourceful and adventurous traveller. There is little doubt that what he saw abroad inspired his interest in community life. He began his journey accompanying Princess Elizabeth Stuart on her journey to Germany, and while they passed through Holland he visited the Anabaptist communities, whose austerity and simplicity of life deeply impressed him. He then broke free of the royal party, travelling on his own over the Alps into Italy, where he lived for two years in Padua, studying medicine at the university. He read avidly the spiritual literature of the Counter-Reformation, such as Francis de Sales' Introduction to the Devout Life. And he must have become familiar with the new religious communities that were springing up, including the Congregation of the Oratory in Padua, a new religious order whose members did not take vows, so as to remind them that their commitment was free and voluntary. Much later at Little Gidding he prevented members of his community from taking vows for similar reasons. From Padua he then went to Spain, where we know little of his movements, and returned to England in 1618. The accounts of his journey show that in the course of it the self-conscious and narrow-minded piety of his adolescent years gave way to an energetic curiosity into every aspect of human affairs. He was fascinated by all kinds of religious rituals and ceremonies, including those of the synagogues in Amsterdam; but also he was constantly inquiring into the commercial and political life of the countries he visited, and took copious notes about the banking system in Hamburg as well as the Holy Week celebrations in Rome.

Little Gidding church interior

On his return Nicholas was offered an academic post in London, and could have resumed his career in Cambridge. But partly out of family duty, and also out of his new-found enjoyment of the affairs of the world, he decided to join the Virginia Company. His father was retiring and although his elder brother John was already a member of the company, his father saw Nicholas as his successor. Nicholas quickly became absorbed in the business, pressing the company to expand its activities in the New World by employing French silk farmers to establish silk production there, in order to export the yarn to England for weaving. He also formed plans to start a university in Virginia, and sent out bibles and financial support for schools. But Nicholas's entrepreneurial flair was partly responsible for King James's growing hostility to the company, because, in threatening the Spanish colonial plans in the New World, it seemed to jeopardize his hope for the Prince of Wales to marry the Spanish Infanta. Almost undoubtedly under Spanish pressure the King set in motion a series of official investigations and interventions in the company's activities which at one point involved Nicholas and his brother being put under house arrest, and which eventually led to the Privy Council closing the company. Nicholas led the company's defence showing himself as a subtle and skilled debater able to present complex arguments clearly and lucidly; he seemed to relish the pressure under which he was forced to work. For a brief period he served in Parliament, not only defending the company from its benches, but also playing a leading role in the impeachment of the Earl of Middlesex, the Lord Treasurer, on charges of bribery and corruption. Middlesex had opposed Nicholas over the Virginia Company, and now Nicholas, in an act of revenge, made a powerful, vitriolic speech for the prosecution.

Despite the collapse of the Virginia Company, Nicholas seemed to have a promising career ahead. His abilities had been noticed, even by his erstwhile opponents, and he was offered two important government posts — a clerkship to the Privy Council and the British ambassadorship in Savoy. And some time earlier a wealthy family friend had offered Nicholas his daughter in marriage, with a handsome dowry. But Nicholas felt increasingly disgusted with himself and his way of life. Although he was not the eldest son, from early childhood his parents' hopes and ambitions had rested on him; and for this reason he was ambitious and proud, always setting himself the highest standards of achievement. However, it also gave him a dread of failure, and a sense of his own unworthiness and inability to live up to such expectations. The cold night spent sobbing in the garden was a childhood manifestation of his capacity for desperate remorse, and his part in Middlesex's condemnation filled him with guilt that haunted him until his death. In the political and commercial world he took easily to positions of authority, and enjoyed his own gifts as a speaker and a leader. But he was fearful of these gifts, as the exercise of them in the world both fed his pride and heightened his fear of failure; and he was painfully embarrassed by the praise and honour heaped upon him.

Thus by early 1625 Nicholas was suffering intense inward turmoil and anguish, and it was in this state of mind that he conceived the idea of a religious community. As a child his greatest satisfaction had been found in precise religious observance; now as an adult a life devoted to religion, in which he could deliberately channel his ambition and energy towards the service of God, increasingly appealed to him as the only means of resolving his inner conflict. Despite his familiarity with both the Anabaptist communities and the Catholic religious orders on the Continent, neither pattern of life was acceptable within an English Church suspicious of both Protestant fanaticism and popery. Thus he decided that the community should be based on a manor house somewhere in the heart of the English countryside, where the ordinary domestic arrangements for such a house could be adapted and sanctified by regular Christian worship. After a brief search he purchased the manor house and nearby chapel at Little Gidding in Huntingdonshire, some 70 miles north of London.

George Herbert

George Herbert was born on 3rd April, 1593, almost an exact contemporary of Nicholas Ferrar. While Ferrar's ancestors had for many centuries been merchants, Herbert's were noblemen and landowners, and he spent his early years at Montgomery Castle, the family home. His father died when George was three, leaving the family with only modest means. His mother Magdalen, a woman of considerable intelligence and wit as well as intense religious devotion, was both strict and highly protective of her children. George idolized her, and from childhood onwards composed Latin verses in her honour, extolling her virtue and artistry. Unlike his elder brother Edward, who was self-confident and assured, George was a shy, anxious child, ambitious for praise yet fearful of ridicule. Even when he was a child his mother wanted him to be a priest, and George was preoccupied throughout his growing years with religion, writing religious poetry and adopting strong doctrinal views.

At the age of 12 George was sent to Westminster School, and four years later went on to Trinity College, Cambridge — where he probably first met Nicholas Ferrar. George was both a snob and a prig. Proud of his noble birth, he regarded most of his fellow students as social inferiors, refusing to make friends with them. And he was contemptuous at what he saw as their loose living. To assert his superiority — and despite lack of funds — he dressed in the most expensive clothes, fit, as he believed, for a nobleman. But he was clever and worked hard, so that after graduating he was invited to be a Fellow of the college, becoming a popular and successful lecturer. He also began to study divinity with

George Herbert

a view to ordination. But in 1619 the post of Public Orator became vacant and he decided to apply. The post carried a considerable income, which he much needed, also prestige, which mattered even more to him, since it involved representing the university to the King and the Court. While outwardly claiming to rely only on his own merits, he used his family connections to secure the post, and so embarked on a short-lived career in public life.

His first task was to heal a rift with King James, who had taken offence at the Cambridge University's failure to organise a ceremony to receive a bound copy of his writings. So George Herbert wrote two letters in Latin to the King, flattering the King's intelligence and virtue, and thereafter became a regular and welcome guest at Court, gaining the special favour of the King's closest friend, the Duke of Lennox. George Herbert soon began to hope for further political advancement, and, partly from personal ambition but also from sincere belief, he strongly and publicly supported the King's plan for a lasting peace with Spain, England's old enemy. But it was this support that eventually thwarted his political career. When the Spanish King broke off negotiations on the marriage of his daughter to Prince Charles, there was a surge of anti-Spanish feeling in Britain, and Prince Charles himself began to advocate war. George Herbert was horrified, and in his role as Public Orator he made a brilliant speech in Prince Charles's presence, condemning the current war fever and urging the cause of peace. A little over a year later King James was dead, and Charles became King; George Herbert's opposition to Charles now meant that his days at Court were over.

In 1624 George Herbert entered Parliament, representing Montgomery, the same town for which his father and elder brother had been elected previously. This was also the election at which Nicholas Ferrar entered Parliament, and he saw Nicholas lose in his attempt to defend the Virginia Company. He stood again in 1625 after King James's death, but by now public life had turned sour for him. After five years in politics his thoughts turned back to religion. He was now a close friend of Nicholas Ferrar, but unlike Nicholas there was no sudden·conversion to a life devoted to God, but another four years of uncertainty and inward preparation. In 1626, the same year that Nicholas was ordained and went to live at Little Gidding, George Herbert was made deacon, and honorary canon of Lincoln Cathedral. The post carried with it the living of Leighton Bromswold, a parish five miles south of Little Gidding, where the Lennox family were lords of the Manor. George Herbert never lived at Leighton, paying a curate to serve in his absence, but its magnificent medieval church captured his imagination. It was in bad repair, with its roof collapsing and its furnishings rotten, and he vowed that one day he would restore it. Soon afterwards he fell ill, and went to live with his brother in Essex.

It was during this period that much of his finest English poetry was written. The only works published in his lifetime were his Latin verses, because his English poetry was written purely for himself, to express privately his inmost feelings. The English poems thus have a directness and simplicity of words and phrase, devoid of rhetorical flourishes, yet also an extraordinary subtlety of form and rhythm. He felt a terrifying sense of disorder and uselessness in his life, and he longed for a clear simple aim in life which would bring peace and order. He was disgusted at his own attachment to both worldly fame and academic achievement, yet was unable to break free. His poetry is full of earthy commonplace images, and even in speaking to God there is no formality, but a straightness and honesty that disarms the reader.

In 1629 he left Essex to live with a stepuncle, Sir John Danvers and his family, who had a large manor house in Wiltshire. Almost immediately he fell in love with Jane, Sir John's third daughter, and in March they married. By now George was stronger, and a year later he was asked to be rector of Bemerton, near Salisbury.

Leighton Bromswold church interior

This was the moment of decision, as moving to Little Gidding had been for Nicholas Ferrar, and for a month he hesitated. He was troubled at the low public esteem in which the country parson was held, and yet, despite his nobility and intelligence, felt unworthy of such a calling. Finally, with Jane's whole-hearted support, he accepted, and was instituted in April 1630; he was ordained priest later that year.

His life as a country parson gave him that clear sense of purpose for which he had longed, and the rhythm of work and worship in the parish brought order and discipline to his restless spirit. Far from despising the mundane concerns of his parishioners, he rejoiced at the simple acts of kindness which he and Jane could perform, with no matter being too trivial for his attention. He wrote a short book entitled 'A Priest to the Temple' in which he described the proper behaviour of the ideal country parson, which he now aspired to become. If the parson is to be respected by his people, he must respect them, however hard-hearted and seemingly indifferent they may be to the things of God: their needs and concerns should become his, and in this way the parson's love of God will inspire his people. Soon George Herbert won the love and admiration of even the farm labourers; and when he and Jane went over to church each morning and evening for prayer, and the church bell was rung, it is said that many of the labourers stopped work for a moment to say a prayer.

George Herbert and Nicholas Ferrar were in regular contact by letter, advising and encouraging each other. George Herbert retained the living of Leighton Bromswold, and decided that he should now restore the church. The Duchess of Lennox gave the necessary money, and George Herbert asked Nicholas and John Ferrar to supervise the work, to be done according to his design. A new roof was put on, and the entire church furnished to the highest standard. The most striking feature was the pulpit and prayer desk at the north and south of the chancel arch: both are of the same height and design, to indicate, contrary to current Puritan opinion, that prayer should be given the same importance as preaching.

The First Community

Forming the Community

Nicholas Ferrar's decision to retire from public life, and to form a household dedicated to God, was personal and private. Yet as soon as the idea formed in his mind he spoke about it with his family. His mother Mary, now a widow, was not only herself devoutly religious, but also highly possessive of her beloved younger son, and the prospect of spending her remaining years with him in a life of quiet devotion readily appealed to her. His elder brother John also decided to join him, along with his wife and children. John's faith was more simple, but no less strong than that of Nicholas, and his decision may have been influenced by his financial situation. He had lost almost his entire inheritance in a dubious business venture which collapsed at the same time as the Virginia Company's demise. More surprisingly, Nicholas Ferrar's elder sister Susanna, a forthright and strong-willed woman, and her husband John Collett, were also enthusiastic. Thus when Nicholas found Little Gidding, and decided that it suited his purpose, it was already clear that his own family would form the core of the community.

In the spring of 1626 the Ferrars began to wind up their affairs in London, and prepare to move. At Easter Nicholas, in the grip of intense religious emotion, began to fast and keep himself awake through the night in order to pray. Eight weeks later on Trinity Sunday, unbeknown to his family, he went to Westminster Abbey to be ordained by Bishop Laud, attended only by his former Cambridge tutor, Linsell. When he returned

Little Gidding church exterior

home to announce his ordination to his family, he took from his breast pocket a sheet of vellum on which he had written a solemn promise to 'separate myself to serve God in his holy calling, to be the Levite in my own house, and to make my own relations, which are many, my cure of souls'.

When the Ferrars bought it the parish of Little Gidding was deserted, apart from a few shepherds' cottages. The original village had died in the Black Death, and the church, long since redundant for worship, was being used as a barn for storing hay, with pigs kept in the vestry. A manor house had been built near the church about a century earlier, but this too was in bad repair. As soon as the purchase was complete, Nicholas employed workmen to restore the house. Soon after the work started he brought his mother to visit Little Gidding for the first time, and she went straight to the church, refusing to set foot in the house until she had offered a prayer of thanksgiving. When she saw the state of the church she was horrified, and told Nicholas to divert the workmen immediately to cleaning and repairing it. She stood outside until sufficient space had been cleared for her to go in and pray. It was a telling incident, for throughout the early years of the community Nicholas's vision and leadership were constantly tempered by his mother's strict sense of good order.

By the time they moved to Little Gidding both church and house were usable, but both drab and undecorated. Thus much of the first five years were devoted to decorating and furnishing, first the church and then the house. Gradually, as things were made ready, other people were able to join the community. Three single men came to act as school masters to the children. A group of rooms were set aside for four elderly widows, who were looked after by the community and who shared in its daily worship. The community also took in teenage boys and young men as part of their education, including one called John Gabbit whose wild behaviour defied even Nicholas's stern discipline.

In addition to Nicholas himself, the personalities who formed the community were for the most part strong-willed and powerful in their various ways, so that learning to live in harmony was a formidable challenge. Mary was over 70 when she arrived at Little Gidding, but despite her age she organised the domestic arrangements of the house. She equalled her son Nicholas both in intelligence and in a taste for rigorous self-discipline. She rose at five in the morning, worked hard through the day, and ate so sparingly during Lent that John had to plead with her to be more lenient with herself. One year she set herself the task of — and succeeded in — learning the entire Psalter by heart.

John Ferrar was a straightforward, guileless man with a strong sense of duty and an easy enjoyment of life. Although older than his brother Nicholas by two years, he admired and looked up to him, often embarrassing Nicholas with lavish praise: in relation to the community he described Nicholas as 'the eye to the body and the soul that giveth life unto it'. His wife, Bathseba, bitterly resented his subservience to Nicholas, and hated the quiet life of the countryside and the monotonous routine of daily worship. She was contemptuous of John and neglectful of their children, and her frequent fits of temper were feared by all in the community.

Susanna, Nicholas's eldest sister, was more of a match for him than their brother John. She willingly argued with him over both community and family matters, curbing his authoritarian instincts, and frustrating some of his wilder plans. She shared the stern piety of Nicholas and their mother, and constantly wrote letters of moral and spiritual advice to friends and relations; but she was saved from unbearable self-righteousness by a sharp sense of irony, often at her own expense. She also shared Nicholas's love of literature and music, and was an accomplished lute player. Her husband, John Collett, was an easy-going ineffectual man who willingly went along with his wife's wishes. He did not share the religious vision that inspired the community but was happy to conform to its requirements.

John and Bathsheba had three children. The eldest son Nicholas, born in 1620, was a brilliant scholar with an exceptional talent for languages. By the age of 14 he had produced a translation of an Italian devotional work which his uncle had brought back from his travels. A few years later he presented to Charles I a Gospel Concordance in four languages, which so impressed the King that he offered to send young Nicholas to Oxford University, and then to employ him in the royal household. Nicholas was shy and spoke with a stammer, a disability he shared with the King, who suggested he tried talking with a pebble in his mouth as a cure. Sadly, young Nicholas, who had always been frail, died suddenly at the age of 20, a few days after meeting the King. John's other two children, Virginia and John, were both born in the community. They lacked any special gifts, but fitted happily into the community's quiet routine, and spent their whole lives at Little Gidding.

By the time she came to Little Gidding, Susanna was in her late 40s and had borne 16 children. Two had died in infancy, and most of the rest had grown up and left home. However the two eldest daughters, Mary and Anna, remained at Little Gidding becoming completely absorbed in the religious life of the community. Mary was in her mid-20s when the family arrived at Little Gidding, and as old Mrs Ferrar declined so Mary came to be regarded as the 'mother' of the community, organising its domestic life. Both she and Anna committed themselves to life-long celibacy, with the support of Nicholas; but Nicholas decided that formal vows were wrong, and that continuous trust in the 'good guidance of their gracious Lord God and Master Jesus Christ' would give sufficient strength.

Worshipping Together

The 17th century was a period of violent religious conflict, not so much over questions of doctrine, but over worship and ritual. High churchmen, led by Bishop Laud and supported by King Charles, loved elaborate liturgies in richly furnished churches; while the Puritans regarded such practices as papist idolatory, preferring an austere, simple form of worship, with strong emphasis on the use of scripture. The Ferrars inclined to the high-church position, but freely adopted Puritan practice as they saw fit.

As soon as they had settled at Little Gidding they established a strict routine of daily worship, according to the Book of Common Prayer. There were thus three main services in the day, each preceding a main meal, and the whole community walked in orderly procession from the house to the church. At 6.30 a.m. there was Morning Prayer, followed by breakfast; at ten there was the Litany, followed by lunch; and at four there was Evening Prayer, followed by supper. In addition, at each hour through the day two or three people held a short service — consisting of a psalm and a reading from the gospels — in the great chamber of the house. Members of the community acquired a familiarity with the Bible which would have been the envy of any Puritan, yet it was Cranmer's liturgy, based on the old monastic practice, which provided the basic framework of worship.

Cranmer had advocated Holy Communion as the main Sunday service, but less than a century later even many high churchmen celebrated communion only a few times a year at major festivals. The Ferrars, however, wanted frequent communion, seeing the sharing of the bread and wine as the very heart of their corporate life. So, on the first Sunday of the month the vicar of Great Gidding, just over a mile away, came to celebrate communion. The position of the communion table was a matter of deep dispute at this time, with Laud and his followers urging it to be placed against the east wall,

Little Gidding altar and brass tablets

like a medieval altar, while the Puritans preferred it brought out into the middle of the chancel, with the people standing round it, to emphasize the fellowship of Christians. In this the Ferrars followed the Puritan practice, since for them as a community it was their close fellowship in Christ they wished primarily to celebrate.

After about five years, in the early 1630s, another discipline of prayer was added, a nightly vigil. Nicholas himself had from the outset yearned for a more contemplative form of prayer than the daily office alone could provide, and as the years passed others in the community came to share this desire. They chose to make the psalms the basis of their nightly prayer, since in the psalms the whole range of human emotions, from depression and anger to love and hope, are expressed openly in prayer, to be sanctified by God. Thus members of the community who wished took it in turns to stay up from nine o'clock to one o'clock, either in church or in the great chamber, and recite the entire Psalter. Then, at the end, they would go and knock at Nicholas's door to wake him, leaving him a lighted candle, and he would spend the remainder of the night in prayer and meditation.

Laud urged people to express the 'beauty of holiness' in their care and decoration of church buildings, and the community at Little Gidding exemplified this. They began by rebuilding the chancel which had fallen down, and then panelled it, installing a narrow bench at the bottom of the panels. This meant that people sat in the church facing one another, creating a sense of intimacy in worship, rather than in rows. At the west end of the church they built a gallery to house a small organ, as music played a central part in their services – in accordance with high-church practice, but against the Puritans' preference. They installed a small brass font, with a lid shaped like a crown, and on the east wall they put three brass tablets, with the Lord's Prayer, the Creed and the Ten Commandments inscribed on them. They also brought from Flanders a brass eagle lectern that had been made in the late 15th century. But to visitors the most striking feature of the church was the rich tapestry and embroidery made by the women of the community. There were two complete sets of decorations, in blue for Sundays, and green for weekdays, embroidered covers for the pulpit and reading desk, velvet cushions for the seats, and floral tapestries to put over the communion table. They also regularly put flowers and herbs picked from their garden to the west of the churchyard, in the church, so that it smelt, as well as looked, sweet.

In 1630, old Mrs Ferrar suggested that members of the community form a study circle, to be called the Little Academy. At first its intention was entirely serious. Nicholas would write a story, usually based on the life of a saint, illustrating some aspect of Christian virtue; and one of the circle would have to learn it by heart and recite it to the rest. But Nicholas was no story-teller, and soon they became bored with this arrangement. Instead they reconstituted themselves, giving each other names that poked gentle fun at one another; and so the violent tempered Bathsheba was named 'Goodwife', and the ineffectual John Collett was called 'Resolved'. At their meetings they took it in turn to tell stories, based on some episode in history or classical mythology, which they collected together in story books. These story books show not only the great breadth of their reading, but also their own moral and political attitudes. The largest of the books contains 34 tales about heroes of the early centuries of the church, the martyrs and desert fathers. Another book has stories from recent European history, including an admiring account of the abdication of Emperor Charles V of Spain, who gave up his throne to devote himself to prayer and charity. Most striking of all is the story of John Frederick, the Elector of Saxony, who refused the offer of a mighty army to recover some of his lost lands. The story-teller speaks of his 'incomparable judgment and abundance of conscience' in preferring peace, even at the loss of earthly power and dignity. The community was thus fully aware of the great political issues of the day, but their way of life gave them a perspective strikingly different to that of most of their contemporaries.

Living Together

The manor house in which the community lived stood about 50 yards to the west of the small church. The approach was up a gentle incline, through a fine grove of trees and shrubs. In the centre of the house was the entrance hall and large parlour, where visitors were received. Nearby was Nicholas's room, where he could talk to visitors and to members of the community in private. A staircase from the parlour led to the great chamber, which was a long gallery, in which the hourly office was said and the nightly vigil kept; in the centre was a table on which a large Bible concordance was kept from which the gospel passages were read. At the other end of the gallery were two rooms set aside for private prayer, one for men and the other for women.

Leading off the great chamber was a large workroom where the Bible concordances were made. Initially at the hourly office an ordinary Bible was used, with one of the four gospels being read through each week. But Nicholas then conceived the idea of a concordance, in which parallel passages from the gospels were placed side by side, so that the life of Christ could be read as a continuous narrative, and the distinctive contributions of each evangelist could be clearly seen. Thus a young woman from Cambridge was brought in to teach them the art of book binding. Copies of the gospels were cut up, and pasted together as Nicholas instructed, and then bound into a single volume. The concordance was divided into 150 chapters, with five chapters to be read each day, and hence the whole book each month. The original intention was to produce only one concordance for their own use, but soon others, who heard of this idea, asked for copies to be made for them, and so it became part of the regular work of the community.

Since his studies in Padua, Nicholas had remained interested in medicine. A room was set aside as an infirmary for members of the community who felt sick, and nearby there was a surgery where local people could come to have their wounds bandaged and to receive simple herbal remedies. This surgery inspired Jane Herbert to start a similar service for their parishioners, and she got from the Ferrars all their herbal recipes. A short distance from the manor house was an old dovecote which had contained several thousand pigeons. The Ferrars decided that keeping pigeons for meat was wrong, since they grew fat by feeding on local farmers' crops, and so the dovecote was converted into a school-room for the community's children. Old Mrs Ferrar presided over the proceedings, sitting on a high-backed chair with the youngest children playing at her feet. The three school masters gave lessons for the older children, one in English and Latin, the second in writing and arithmetic, and the third in singing and music.

The whole community, including the children, ate their meals together. At the start of each meal they sang a short hymn, and while they ate, one of the older children read aloud, having eaten earlier. Unlike the traditional monastery they avoided religious books, preferring instead biographies, history books and travel diaries, in order to broaden their knowledge of the affairs of the world. The community also provided a simple meal each morning for any travellers or local people — many of whom were poor — who wished to come; and they took food to those who were sick in the neighbour-hood. Under the overall supervision of old Mrs Ferrar, and later under Mary Ferrar, the unmarried women of the community took it in turns, for a month at a time, to organize the cooking and the cleaning of the house.

The leadership of the community evolved over the years. At the beginning Nicholas made the decisions and gave the orders. Although he had no manual skills, he was fascinated by the most mundane aspects of daily life, and could readily understand practical problems. In the early years he frequently intervened in the organisation of every aspect of the community's work, and he supervised its financial affairs. He was an authoritarian leader, confident in the decisions he made, and so in the formative years he was responsible for establishing the community's pattern of life. But as things became more settled he gradually withdrew from day-to-day affairs, handing the practical leadership of the community to his elder brother John and to Mary. Nicholas's role changed to that of adviser and pastor. Members of the community frequently came to him, both to talk over practical issues and also for spiritual direction. Receiving his help was neither comfortable nor easy. He would listen carefully, asking sharp and penetrating questions, and then, when he understood matters to his satisfaction, he would give clear and firm advice. People could accept his wisdom and spiritual authority because he ruled his own life by a far stricter discipline than he would ever impose on others. And his love and concern for the well-being of every individual in the community was beyond question.

Friends and Enemies

When he came to Little Gidding Nicholas severed all his connections with the social and public life of London, in which he had become well known, and deliberately sought obscurity. Nonetheless Little Gidding soon began to attract numerous visitors, and the Ferrars became far more famous in the remote countryside than they ever were in the city. They welcomed visitors warmly, enjoying their company and the news they brought of the affairs of the world, but the community was in danger of having the quiet, industrious order of its life swamped by the demands of hospitality. And, in a period when the country was torn by religious and political strife, there was the constant threat of spies whose purpose would be to spread false rumour and scandal.

They therefore developed a strict rule of hospitality. Only friends, or those recommended by friends, were allowed to stay in the community. Strangers were given a glass of wine or tankard of ale, their questions were answered briefly but honestly, and then they were sent on their way. They were not asked to stay for a meal or for the night, and this caused some offence to people of noble birth who had expected a more lavish welcome. The only exceptions to this were tramps in need of food, and they were invited into the kitchen for a meal; this prompted some visitors to dress up as tramps to get a closer look at the community. A brass tablet, which expressed the community's attitude, was put up over the chimney piece in the parlour where visitors were received. Its words were composed by George Herbert, on old Mrs Ferrar's instructions:

IHS

He who (by reproof or our errors and remonstrance of that which is more perfect), and seeks to make us better, is welcome as an angel of God.

He who (by a cheerful participation and approbation of that which is good) confirms us in the same, is welcome as a Christian friend.

but

He who in any way goes about to disturb us in that which is and ought to be amongst Christians (Tho it be not usual in and the world) is a burden while he stays and shall bear his judgement, whosoever he be.

He who faults us in absence for that which in presence he makes show to approve of, doth by a double guilt of flattery and slander violate the bonds both of friendship and charity.

Leighton Bromswold church rainwater head

During his travels Nicholas had come to admire many aspects of Roman Catholicism, especially the new religious orders such as the Jesuits who had sprung up in the 16th century; and, although firmly Protestant in his convictions, he was eager to maintain contacts with the small, often persecuted, Roman Catholic community in England. It was too dangerous for Catholic priests and Jesuits to stay at Little Gidding itself, but fortunately Katherine Clifton, now Duchess of Lennox, allowed Nicholas's Roman Catholic contacts to stay at her lodge at Leighton Bromswold, from where they were discreetly brought over to Little Gidding to see Nicholas. At these meetings Nicholas debated the major points of theological dispute between Protestants and Catholics in the hope of finding common ground, and he became much admired by Catholics for his understanding of their position. Katherine Clifton was a devout Roman Catholic, and her father Sir Gervais Clifton had been imprisoned in the Tower of London for his beliefs, and had died there. But she, like Nicholas, deeply desired reconciliation between Catholics and Protestants, even allowing her lodge to be used for Anglican services while George Herbert was restoring the church at Leighton Bromswold.

The poet Richard Crashaw, who later became a Roman Catholic, was a regular visitor to Little Gidding in the early 1630s. He was a man of frenzied emotion who grieved what he regarded as the spiritual and aesthetic impoverishment that the Reformation had brought on the Church of England. He was both saintly and sensuous, longing for the mystical spirituality and colourful ritual of the medieval church. He first came to Little Gidding when he was a student at Cambridge, and was enthralled by the monastic devotion of the community. Mary Collett in particular captured his heart, and he wrote a poem in honour of 'this holy woman' in her 'friar's grey gown', who was the 'gentlest, kindest, most tender-hearted and liberal-handed soul I think is today alive'. When Nicholas introduced the nightly vigils Richard Crashaw often came over from Cambridge to join the vigil; and when Crashaw became curate at Little St Mary's Church in Cambridge he introduced a similar practice there. His poetry contains a number of references to Little Gidding, and one poem, dedicated to a 'religious house' describes the community beautifully:

. . . Our lodgings hard and homely as our fare,
That chaste and cheap, as the few clothes we wear;
Those, coarse and negligent, as the natural locks
Of these loose groves; rough as th' unpolished rocks.
A hasty portion of prescribed sleep;
Obedient slumbers, that can wake and weep,
And sing, and sigh, and work, and sleep again;
Still rolling a round sphere of still-returning pain.
Hands full of hearty labours; pains that pay
And prize themselves; do much, that more they may,
And work for work, not wages; let to-morrow's
New drops wash off the sweat of this day's sorrows.
A long and daily-dying life, which breathes
A respiration of reviving deaths.
But neither are there those ignoble stings
That nip the blossom of the World's best things,
And lash Earth-labouring souls.
No cruel guard of diligent cares, that keep
Crown'd woes awake, as things too wise for sleep:
But reverent discipline, and religious fear,
And soft obedience, find sweet biding here;
Silence, and sacred rest; peace, and pure joys;
Kind loves keep house, lie close, and make no noise;
And room enough for monarchs, while none swells
Beyond the kingdom of contentful cells.
The self-rememb'ring soul sweetly recovers
Her kindred with the stars; not basely hovers
Below: but meditates her immortal way
Home to the original source of Light and intellectual
    day.

The most distinguished — and ultimately most dangerous — friend of the community was King Charles. His first contact came in the early 1630s when he was staying a few miles away at Apethorpe, the home of the Earl of Westmorland. He was told of the gospel concordance that the community had made for their hourly prayers, and sent a messenger to Little Gidding to ask to borrow it. The King kept it for some months, using it in his own devotions. He wrote various notes in the margin, suggesting improvements to the text, one of which he carefully crossed out, writing below: 'I confess my error; it was well before. I was mistaken.' His queen, Henrietta Maria, a Roman Catholic, also heard of the community, and was planning a visit until she learnt that the road there was very bumpy. Instead she sent a courtier, who impressed her with his account of 'a Protestant family that outdid the severest monastics abroad'.

When the King returned the concordance he asked that one like it be produced for him within 12 months. This was done and when John Ferrar presented it to the King he described it as 'a rich and rare jewel', declaring: 'How happy a king were I, if I had many more such workmen and women in my kingdom. God's blessing on their hearts and painful hands.' He then asked for a similar concordance of the books of Kings and Chronicles from the Old Testament. In his frequent readings of the books he said he had found 'some seeming contradiction', and hoped that by seeing parallel passages put together this might be resolved. He complained that 'I have often spoken to many of my chaplains about this thing, but they have excused themselves from it as a difficult work'. So the community set to work on this book, and presented it to the King a year later. Then the King asked for a gospel concordance for his son, Prince Charles, which John Ferrar's son, Nicholas, produced.

The King visited Little Gidding in March 1642, accompanied by Prince Charles Louis, only five months before the outbreak of the Civil War. He was on his way northwards to secure a northern port, to ensure that, if necessary, he could receive military help from the Continent; and it is extraordinary that at such a fearful time the King could quietly spend a day with a religious community. After being shown the chapel, the King spent some hours studying a copy of the Pentateuch, which the community had produced and bound, before visiting the widows cared for by the community. He gave them five golden coins — it was, he declared, the only money he had with him, having won it at cards the previous evening! Meanwhile the Prince and the court-iers were being fed apple pie and cheesecake by the community. At sunset the King mounted his horse to leave, and the whole community knelt down nearby, praying for God's blessing on him. The King took off his hat, and begged the community: 'Pray, pray for my speedy and safe return again.'

Nicholas Ferrar's contacts with the Roman Catholic Church, and the community's friendship with the King, made them highly vulnerable to destructive Puritan zeal. Even in the 1630s a story gained wide circulation that there were 12 crosses in the east window of the church, and that members of the community bowed to these crosses when they entered. The origin of the story was that the window had three upright iron bars and four horizontal ones, and someone had mischievously suggested that the intersections of the bars were crosses. But such was the eagerness of people to believe such rumours that it was soon taken seriously, and visitors to the community began to inquire about it.

Far more damaging was the publication in 1641 of a pamphlet about Little Gidding entitled 'The Arminian Nunnery, or a Briefe Description and Relation of the Late Erected Monasticall Place'. The term 'Arminian', though it had a theological meaning referring to the teaching of a Dutch theologian, was in the context a general term of abuse, being, as the pamphlet said, 'a bridge to Popery'. On the cover was a rough woodcut of a woman in nun's habit with a rosary in her hand.

THE
ARMINIAN
NVNNERY:

OR,

A BRIEFE DESCRIPTION

and Relation of the late erected *Monasticall* Place, called the ARMINIAN NVNNERY at little GIDDING in HVNTINGTON-SHIRE.

Humbly recommended to the wise consideration of this present PARLIAMENT.

The Foundation is by a Company of FARRARS at *GIDDDING.*

'Arminian Nunnery' title page

The pamphlet was based on a letter by Edward Lenton, who had visited the community some years previously; but it grossly distorted Lenton's description. It referred to the members 'crouching, cringing and prostrating to the ground to the altar-like communion table, or the rich gilded candlesticks', and to their 'promiscuous private prayers all the night long'. The pamphlet was widely circulated, and was submitted 'to the wise consideration of this present parliament', implying that Parliament should take steps to close the community. Lenton himself was appalled by the misuse of his letter by 'such hucksters', and John Ferrar described it 'as stuffed with abominable falsehoods and such stories as the devil himself would be ashamed to utter'.

Parliament did not in fact act on the pamphlet, but the notoriety it gave to Little Gidding meant that throughout the Civil War the community lived in fear of attack. They survived unmolested throughout the hostilities, but at the very end they were forced to pay dearly for their personal loyalty to the King. On 2nd May, 1646, King Charles, defeated and alone, wandering aimlessly around eastern England, arrived at Little Gidding during the night seeking refuge. Fearing that the Parliamentary troops might come and search for him at Little Gidding, John Ferrar took him to a private house in Coppingford about four miles away. The King left the following morning, and was arrested shortly afterwards. A few weeks later, in reprisal for harbouring the King, Parliamentary troops ransacked the church and house. The community had received warning of their approach, and were able to flee. The troops wrecked the interior of the church, ripping out the organ and gallery and burning them in the churchyard, and roasted six of the community's sheep on the fires. The brass font and the eagle lectern were thrown into a pond nearby.

Once the danger had passed, the community returned to Little Gidding. For a further 11 years they continued their routine of daily worship, but they left the church unrepaired, fearful that if they restored it to its earlier glory they would invite further Puritan attack.

End and Beginning

Early in 1633 news arrived in Little Gidding that George Herbert was seriously ill and unlikely to recover. Nicholas immediately asked a friend, Edmund Duncan, to travel to Bemerton to convey a message of love and to get first-hand news. When Duncan arrived, George Herbert handed him a little book to take to Nicholas, asking him to read it, and either to publish or burn it as Nicholas saw fit. George Herbert died on 1st March, and, with a short preface by himself, Nicholas published the book. It contained George Herbert's English poems, hitherto unread by anyone, and during the next 30 years sold 20,000 copies; many of the poems were subsequently set to music, and are amongst the finest and most popular hymns in the English language.

In the summer of 1637, five years after George Herbert's death, Nicholas became ill with the same 'ague' which had regularly affected him in his younger days. Although the immediate crisis passed quickly, it left him severely depressed, and his usual courage and enthusiasm deserted him. By the autumn his spirits had recovered, but he was now convinced he was dying. In late October he shocked his brother John by telling him, 'I am shortly to appear before my good Lord'. He entrusted the future of the community to John's hand, urging him to maintain strictly their existing way of life: 'It is the right, good, old way you are in; keep in it. God will be worshipped in spirit and truth, in body and in soul, He will have both inward love and fear, and outward reverence of body and gesture. You, I say, know the way; keep in it: I will not use more words, you have lessons enow given you; be constant to them.' Nicholas believed that the religious and political conflicts of the country would grow worse, and he warned John, 'there will be sad times to come, and very sad,' and that 'you will be sifted, and endeavour will be made to turn you out of the right way, the good way you are in, even by those whom you least think of'.

Shortly after this conversation, when he had digested what his brother had said, John returned in great distress, wondering how they could possibly cope if Nicholas should die — 'if the shepherd be thus now taken from us'. In a flash of anger Nicholas rebuked John for his feebleness, ordering him to 'go to church, and fast this day, and beg God to forgive you'. A few weeks later Nicholas fell ill again. He told the community he was now ready to die, the desire to recover and live having left him. He also asked them to take the large number of books from his room, and burn them in the churchyard. These were plays and stories he had collected during his travels but now he felt ashamed of his attachment to them, and so this invaluable library was destroyed.

By Advent Sunday he was close to death, and through the day he constantly repeated the first verse of the 70th Psalm: 'Haste thee, O Lord, to deliver me: make haste to help me, O Lord.' In the evening he fell into a peaceful sleep, with the whole family gathered at his bedside. Then, at one o'clock on the following morning, 4th December, he suddenly raised himself up in bed, stretched out his arms, looked upwards, and spoke in a clear, strong voice: 'O, what blessed change is here. What do I see? O, let us come and sing unto the Lord, sing praises to the Lord and magnify his holy name together. I have been at a great feast. O magnify the Lord with me!' His niece Mary questioned him: 'A feast, dear father?' 'Aye,' he answered, 'at a great feast, a great King's feast.' He then sank quietly back in his bed, and died.

While it was Nicholas whose vision had established the community, it was the steady hand of John, loyally supported by Mary and Anna, which carried the community through the traumatic years of the Civil

Little Gidding font

War. In 1657 John and his sister, Susanna, died within a few months of each other, and the manor house passed to John's eldest surviving son, also called John. While proud of his father's and uncle's achievement, John desired for himself only the life of a country squire. Thus the old pattern of daily prayer was abandoned. John did, however, renovate the church some decades later in 1714, pulling down the nave which had almost collapsed, and building a new nave and west front to match the chancel built by the community; he also rescued the font and lectern from the pond, and restored them to the church.

In the two and a half centuries after John and Susanna's deaths, the story of Little Gidding evoked little interest except among historians of the period. Community life was not a major concern of the Church, so Little Gidding seemed little more than an eccentric experiment. The church at Little Gidding was also neglected until William Hopkinson purchased the manor in 1848, restoring the church with a mixture of Victorian vulgarity and inspired good taste. The Ferrar's manor house had burnt down some decades earlier, and Hopkinson built a large farmhouse in its place.

In the late 19th century the revival of monastic life in the Church of England stimulated fresh appreciation of the Ferrar community. The founders of the new religious houses saw Little Gidding as evidence of a continuing English tradition of community life that had survived the Reformation. One such community, the Oratory of the Good Shepherd, was founded at Little Gidding church in 1913. The Oratory is a non-residential community of priests, and they chose Little Gidding in which to take their vows because of Nicholas Ferrar's contact with the original Oratory of Philip Neri in Italy.

It was, however, the middle decade of the 20th century that saw a widespread re-awakening of interest in Little Gidding. As Christians throughout the world began to explore the renewal of community life for families as well as for single people, many found inspiration in the story of the Ferrars. Little Gidding became a place of pilgrimage; and one such pilgrim, T. S. Eliot, gave it greater fame than it had ever enjoyed in the 17th century. His poem 'Little Gidding', published in 1942, is a prolonged and profound meditation on the spirit of the community. Its recurring image is that of fire: Christian life, exemplified by the Ferrars is a painful struggle to be freed from one fire, the passionate attachment to worldly things, by the fire of Christ's redeeming love, which alone can bring peace:

In 1947 the Friends of Little Gidding was formed, supported by T. S. Eliot. The founder was Alan Maycock, librarian of Magdalene College, Cambridge, who in 1938 had published a biography of Nicholas Ferrar. The purpose of the Friends was to raise funds for the maintenance of Little Gidding church, once again falling into decay, and to organise an annual pilgrimage there. But Maycock, in the conclusion of his book, wrote of his hope that one day Little Gidding 'will belong to a community who will pass to and from the church for the daily offices, following the "good old way" of devotion to the service of God and their fellow men'. This vision was eventually realised, but the process was long and tortuous.

In 1969 a group of people from amongst the Friends formed the Little Gidding Fellowship, meeting each week to pray for the renewal of community life at or near Little Gidding. Remarkably, a year later the farmhouse near the church, with outbuildings and seven acres of land, came on the market, and one couple in the fellowship, Tony and Judith Hodgson, were able to purchase it. The original intention had been to convert the outbuildings into houses for other members of the group and so form a community. But tensions and divisions amongst them prevented this, and in 1973 the Hodgsons moved there alone to run it as a small Christian conference centre and hostel. Two years later Veronica Grey, a retired bursar of a theological college, joined them to look after the accounts and administration. Tony and Judith Hodgson, with their two young daughters, had to live in the farmhouse as there was no other accommodation, and they devoted themselves without rest to the needs of the guests. Soon the strain on their family became unbearable, and in 1976 they decided to leave and sell the property.

My wife Sarah and I had been visiting Little Gidding periodically throughout these years. Even as a child I dreamt of living in a community, and my interest in Little Gidding was first awakened while still a teenager, when, by chance, I picked up Alan Maycock's book from a secondhand stall in London: the story, and his vision of the rebirth of community at Little Gidding, captured my imagination. Observing the numerous experiments in community life springing up all over Britain — and indeed throughout the world — I was aware that the great majority collapsed after only a few short years, often leaving a debris of broken marriages and lost fortunes. So we began to study closely how monasteries work, to see what clues they could offer, and we spent a year in Ethiopia exploring monastic life there. When the property at Little Gidding again came up for sale, we felt ready to commit ourselves wholeheartedly to community life, hoping that the lessons learnt from the monastic tradition would enable us to create a stable form of community life for families. We borrowed money from a building society to enable a charitable trust to purchase the house and smallholding at Little Gidding; and in the summer of 1977, with a heavy mortgage to pay, we moved in, with Veronica Grey staying on to share the new venture.

Friends of Little Gidding

The Society of the Friends of Little Gidding was founded in 1946—

(1) as an act of thanksgiving to Almighty God for the holy lives and examples of Nicholas Ferrar and those who shared in his life at Little Gidding.

(2) to venerate his memory and to honour those ideals of Christian family life of which Little Gidding provided so perfect a pattern.

(3) to take a practical and active interest in the care, upkeep and adornment of the church of Little Gidding and its precincts.

(4) to arrange, as occasion provides, for visits and pilgrimages to Little Gidding and, in any other ways that may be deemed fitting, to preserve the sense of Little Gidding as a holy place, from which the sanctity can never depart.

Friends' Report 1952-3

The Second Community

Forming the Community

When we arrived at Little Gidding we had almost no money and were unable to pay the bills on the large house. There were only three adults to look after the place, one of whom, Veronica, was almost 70 years of age, and another, my wife Sarah, was absorbed in looking after our two small children.

We found ourselves in a vicious circle caused by the lack of living accommodation. On the one hand, until we had more people we could not generate the income to build new houses; and on the other, without new houses we could not attract additional people. To meet the immediate bills I decided to seek a job, and became a lecturer in economics in Cambridge; but while this saved us from bankruptcy, it only made the shortage of labour to care for Little Gidding even more acute. We were able to allocate two rooms in the farmhouse for guests, and this provided some additional income, but also, of course, caused more work. We were also able to accommodate two young volunteers, and their work enabled us to keep the site clean and tidy. But at times during the first two years we almost despaired of ever being able to form a community, since the situation was so uncertain and the work so hard that no sensible person would consider joining us.

Nicholas Ferrar's experience in business and his entrepreneurial spirit were essential for the founding of the first community, and it was soon clear to us that we should take the same risks in starting a new community as a business man would in starting a new firm. The old farm buildings near the house included an ancient timber structure, which may have served as a shed in the Ferrars' day, but was now covered in rusty corrugated iron, and slowly collapsing. We sought planning permission for this to be converted into four houses, and we commissioned a local architect to draw plans, and to obtain quotations from builders. With the Charity Commissioners' approval we set up a loan fund into which people would put money to finance the houses; they would not get interest, but the loan could be linked to the value of the houses. I also persuaded our bank to offer a loan equal to half the building costs. This was the maximum they were prepared to lend, and even this required me to juggle with figures to mislead the bank manager as to our ability to repay. So, in February 1980, building work started and, unbeknown to the builder and architect, we were praying that the loan fund would attract sufficient money during the coming months to enable us to meet the costs.

This act of faith in building houses inspired sufficient confidence for people to contribute money, and, as things turned out, the bank loan was unnecessary. One young couple, David and Heather Sherlock, who had been wondering whether to join, decided to sell their house and put the proceeds in the loan fund. A number of well-wishers made loans, encouraged by the fact that rising house prices made it a reasonable investment. The balance was made up by an inheritance that I unexpectedly received. Once the houses were built the vicious circle was broken, as new people could now join.

Those who came in the following six or seven years fell into two categories: single people, either unmarried or widowed, mostly in late middle-age; and young families with children not yet at school, and so with no strong ties to an existing home. The single people settled relatively easily, but the families found it more difficult; and three families, including the Sherlocks, came and went within three years. In each case there were different reasons. For one family it was the problems within their

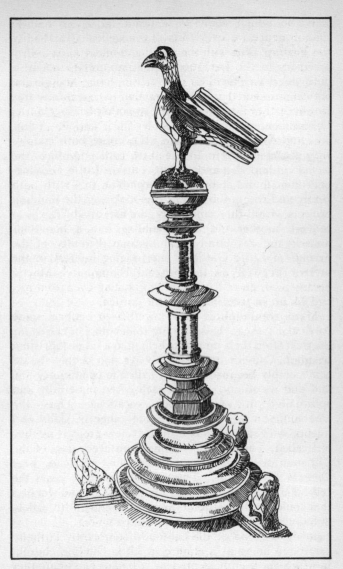

Little Gidding lectern

marriage which came to a head; for another their commitment to a strict form of evangelical Christianity was incompatible with the moral and material flexibility necessary in the formation of a community; and for a third the desire for their own private home and garden proved stronger than their attraction to community life. However, they were followed by two other families whose commitment proved more stable: Chris and Pat Saunders and Martin and Maureen Leverton, both couples with young children. In the three earlier families, the husbands had demanding jobs outside Little Gidding, and often found it difficult to combine this with both family and community life. Chris took over the building projects within the community, the first of which was to convert another old farm building into a home for himself and his family. Pat became secretary of the Friends of Little Gidding, encouraging interest in the present as well as the original community. Martin became warden of Little Gidding, taking over from me, and Maureen took charge of the garden.

Many communities come together to perform some particular task, such as running conferences or caring for the sick; often their members belong to a single Christian tradition. Our intention was always that people should come simply because they felt called to community life, and that we should support each other, materially and spiritually, in our various vocations. Thus the community now contains a wide range of skills and talents, with members free to start new projects as they feel called. The members come from every part of the Christian spectrum: Roman Catholic, Anglican, Free Church, and Quaker. Thus in our formative years the central challenge was to find a pattern of life and worship that could bind together a mixture of people with widely differing vocations and spiritual experiences.

In the autumn of 1981 the new community formally came into being at a service in Little Gidding church, in which the members made a covenant one to another before God. We adopted the name the Community of

Christ the Sower, and we took upon ourselves a simple rule of life.

Worshipping Together

Alongside building a firm financial foundation for the community, the most important task we faced from the outset was developing the right pattern of worship. The first Little Gidding community simply adopted the Book of Common Prayer, but for a modern ecumenical community there was no suitable prayer book available. We were forced to consider the most basic questions: how often should we worship together, and what form of service should we use; and whether we should celebrate communion, as, at that time, Anglicans and Catholics sharing the bread and the wine was against the rules of both denominations.

For daily prayer we decided at first to use the Taize office, since the Taize community have been pioneers in ecumenical forms of worship. The daily office, developed for use within a monastery, stipulates two main services each day, in the morning and the evening; and for a brief period we tried to have both services. But we soon realized that it was only feasible to meet in the early morning since, for young families, evening prayer was constantly disrupted by the vagaries of children's needs; indeed, it was not until we had two alternative times for morning prayer that everyone could meet, as both parents could not leave their children at the same time. Thus we used only the Taize morning service, leaving families or informal groups of single people to have their own forms of worship in the evening to suit their particular needs.

For the first few months we had no regular Communion service at all. I was not yet ordained (later in 1981 I became an Anglican priest), but quite apart from that it seemed wrong to celebrate Communion according to the rules and rites of a particular denomination. Yet we felt that for a Christian community not to share bread and wine would be like a marriage which was unconsummated. So we decided to look for a form of service that had no denominational links, and, regardless of the rules, to start celebrating Communion, taking it in turns to preside. We adopted a rite composed for an ecumenical church in New York, and, with considerable trepidation, we began to celebrate Communion every Saturday evening leaving people free to go to their denominational churches on Sunday morning. Almost at once we were sure that our decision had been right, and even those from the Catholic tradition who had initially doubted the validity of such a service were quickly convinced that it was indeed a true Communion. Moreover, the sharing of the presidency amongst members of the community seemed to reflect the shared mutual ministry on which community life depends.

Within a year or two, however, we began to feel dissatisfied with the forms of service we were using. They were too complex, suited to a large congregation in church, but not to a small informal group, and they were too wordy, leaving insufficient times for silence and free prayer. So, over a period of five years, we composed our own prayer book, which was published eventually in 1986. Both the main services — the Daily Prayer and the Communion — are as simple as possible while still preserving the traditional ingredients of such services. The main innovation in the Daily Service is a new Psalter, using poetry drawn from throughout the Old and New Testaments. In compiling it I was astonished at the rich variety of poetic imagery and the profound mystical insights to be found in almost every book of the Bible. Composing the Communion service required me first to study the traditional liturgies of the various churches, in order to include within our service all the traditional aspects of a celebration of communion. Then, using, as far as possible, phrases from the New Testament, I tried to write a service which conformed precisely to the liturgical traditions, and yet was direct and simple. This proved far more difficult than I had anticipated, and I composed at least seven different services before discovering the form of service that seemed appropriate to our needs. The process of composing the services taught us that worship within a community needs a quite different style to that of formal church worship. Whereas a church service must to some degree be a form of drama, in which quite elaborate words and actions can be appropriate, such an approach quickly becomes stale and lifeless within a community. Simple words and actions, with long periods of silence, are necessary if worship is to be sustained, day by day and week by week, by a close-knit group of people.

In addition to the main services we also developed four special annual services. The first, taking place in early autumn, is a Covenant service at which we renew our commitments to the community, and new members join. The second, usually at Epiphany, marks our common stewardship of time and money within the community: people lay gifts at the Lord's table symbolising some aspect of their daily work — a tool, an account book or whatever. The third, during Lent, is a service of healing, in which hands are laid on each member as a sign that all of us stand in need of God's reconciling love. And the fourth, usually at the Feast of St Peter, is a form of ordination in which everyone is commissioned for their various spiritual ministries within the community, again by laying on of hands.

Living Together

The moment when we began to design the houses at Little Gidding was terrifying. We realised that the decisions that we were about to make, based on intuition rather than experience, would affect the life of the community for decades to come — and could not be reversed. The layout of the community's buildings affect to a considerable degree its spirit. Communities of

53

Little Gidding community courtyard

families living in one large house divided into flats often feel, psychologically as well as physically, that they are living on top of each other. So we decided that families should each have their own house; and the front doors should lead into a garden so that children could wander out and play without danger. The old farm buildings formed the shape of a courtyard; and, although some were so dilapidated that they had to be demolished, we decided to retain this basic plan.

Far more complex questions arose, however, when we started to plan the interior of the houses. We needed to predict what rooms and facilities a family in a community would require, and also to cater for families of different sizes — and for the possibility of a family having more children after they have joined the community. We decided that each house should have one large living room, in which the family could eat as well as relax together; these rooms should also be large enough to hold meetings. We also decided that the houses would need only small kitchens, since most of the food storage would be done in the communal house. However, the basic problem came in determining the number of bedrooms. We felt that once a family had settled in a house they should not be required to move, simply because their house might be more suitable for a new family, or because their children had grown up and left home; instead a family should feel secure, so that they could regard their particular house as their family home. In the first block of four houses we overcame this problem by putting between each pair of houses two additional bedrooms and a bathroom; these could be flats for single people, each with a separate front door, or by connecting doors they could be incorporated into either house, depending on family needs. In subsequent building, where the houses have been detached, this flexibility has not been possible, and we have decided that it is better to risk wasting rooms than for families to feel squashed.

While accommodating families poses one set of questions, housing single people within a community presents a quite different challenge. Some single people want the independence that a family needs, with an entirely self-contained house or flat, while others enjoy a more communal setting, sharing a kitchen and sitting room. Also from the outset we wanted Little Gidding to include people at every stage of life. Not only should young families flourish, but people should be able to grow old and die in comfort. Thus in addition to family houses, we realised that two other kinds of accommodation had to be provided. First, small houses or flats that would be sufficient for a single person or couple without children; and secondly, large rooms for single people, within a single house. For the latter the upper two storeys of the old farmhouse were converted into four large bed-sitting rooms, with shared kitchens and bathrooms.

The ground floor of the farmhouse is the focal point of the community. In a parish weekly worship is the main corporate activity, so the church building is the hub of Christian life. In a community we eat, work and relax, as well as worship together, so a large, rambling house is the ideal focus of our life. As the community has grown in size, so the use of the farmhouse has changed and numerous alterations have been made. At first, when there was only a small group, we cooked and ate together every day, so we needed a large kitchen; but, since even with visitors we rarely numbered more than a handful, our chapel could be an old boxroom at the top of the house. Now people cook for themselves, so the farmhouse kitchen is small and used mainly for making drinks and snacks, but we need a far larger chapel, so the old parlour has been converted for this purpose. We also need a large larder, since we purchase — and produce — the basic foods communally.

In establishing a stable pattern of life, two issues proved crucial — the stewardship of money and material resources, and leadership within the community. Many communities founder because, inspired by the Jerusalem church, they pool all their money and resources. While the spirit behind such a system is right, in practice it quickly proves unwieldy (as the Jerusalem church found) and often very damaging to family life. The community has to establish a central administration to make all material decisions, and as a consequence families lose their natural independence. So, following the practice of the Ethiopian monastery, we decided that each of us should make a detailed annual review of our stewardship. Thus every year a community budget is drawn up, estimating both the financial needs and the work required within the community. Each family and single person then draws up a personal budget of their use of time and money, seeking to balance the demands of both family and community. A pastor of the community talks in confidence with each household, going through their budget in detail, including what they intend to contribute to the community. Finally we check whether the total of members' contributions will meet the community's needs. This system has proved remarkably successful, both in preserving the freedom of families and individuals, and yet encouraging a generous attitude to money and time. The annual meeting with a pastor compels us each to work out clearly and deliberately the material implications of our faith, that we are stewards, not owners, of God's gifts.

When Nicholas Ferrar founded the first community, he alone had authority over every aspect of its life, but gradually, as it became established, others took charge of different spheres, and he withdrew. This meant that after his early death others were able to lead and sustain the community through its most difficult years. In the same way in the early years of the new community I took decisions in every sphere of our life, down to the smallest practical details, and almost nothing happened without my knowledge and approval. To some outside observers, and indeed to some of the young volunteers, I was unduly dictatorial; and I made innumerable mistakes, great and small. Yet both Sarah and Veronica wholly supported me, patiently enduring my mistakes,

Little Gidding hour-glass stand

knowing that only through such clear and firm leadership could our enormous initial problems be overcome. But as soon as the new houses were built and others came, I gradually handed over responsibility for different aspects of our life, as the gifts and inclinations of the newcomers allowed.

As we had originally intended, the pattern of leadership that finally emerged – as with our system of stewardship – is similar to that of the Ethiopian monastery. The whole community appoints pastors by unanimous consent — and this, plus the acceptance of new members, are the only decisions made by the whole community. The pastors are guides and advisers, with the ability to discern and encourage the gifts of others; they in turn appoint managers to look after each different aspect of the community's life. There is thus, as in the Ethiopian monastery, a clear distinction between spiritual direction and practical management, but the two types of leaders will work in harmony and mutual trust since the pastors choose the managers. The system ensures great flexibility in our organisation, since the structure of management can readily be changed as circumstances alter. To outsiders, accustomed to modern democracy in which decisions are taken by votes, and authority exercised through committees, the community can seem authoritarian. Yet, by putting our trust in individuals rather than systems, decisions are made with far greater sensitivity to people's needs and feelings. Moreover the faction-forming and politicking that democracy encourages is absent, since it brings no reward; only by striving towards unity can people influence decisions.

Outwards and Inwards

Nicholas Ferrar's and George Herbert's experiments in community were linked but separate — Nicholas Ferrar's in a Huntingdonshire manor house, and George

Herbert's in a Wiltshire village. From the start we hoped that these two patterns of life would, in our case, be incorporated into one community: that the Community of Christ the Sower would include both those in a residential group at Little Gidding, and also members scattered in ordinary parishes, all living according to the same rule of life. Indeed, as we framed our rule, although at that time all members were living at Little Gidding, we tried to ensure that it would be equally suitable for a group of people in a village or town.

The way in which we found ourselves drawn outwards from Little Gidding was unplanned and unexpected – but confirmed our conviction that the community should spread to ordinary parishes. The first stage came following my ordination in 1981. Almost immediately afterwards the vicar of the surrounding group of parishes left, and I was asked regularly to take services in the churches. Until then local people had naturally regarded developments at Little Gidding with some bewilderment and even suspicion, but my increasing involvement with the parish churches helped to reduce this. And a year later the parishes themselves asked Peter Walker, the Bishop of Ely, to make me their vicar. Peter Walker had been a very good and loving friend to us since we came to Little Gidding; and now, although I had not served a curacy and my formal training had been scanty, he waived the normal rules. So, in January 1983, I was instituted as parish priest. At my request I did not receive a salary, but retained my job as a lecturer.

My appointment as parish priest led in turn to the first outward movement of the community. Since the group at Little Gidding was still so new, it seemed essential that for the time being I should remain living there. But this meant that the large old vicarage at Great Gidding was available, and the diocese leased it to the community. We divided it into two self-contained houses and a young married couple, Peter and Louise Burrows, moved into the main part. The other part was available for people who wished to live temporarily within the

Leighton Bromswold church exterior

community. Thus the first household of the community outside Little Gidding was formed.

The second stage of our spreading outwards cemented our spiritual bond with George Herbert. Although he never lived at Leighton Bromswold, the church there, restored by him with the Ferrars' help, embodies his vision of parish spirituality. By early 1985 I was aware that the community at Little Gidding was nearing its maximum size, since further expansion there would jeopardize its intimacy and informality; thus, if we were to remain open to new members, it was essential that another group be formed elsewhere.

Reflecting on this I had a strong, and quite unexpected, premonition that an old house near Leighton church, that I had seen through the trees, would be the centre of a new group. Apart from mentioning this to Sarah and a few others, I thought nothing more of it. Then in the autumn of that year we heard through friends that the present owners of the house were about to offer it for sale. I went to visit it, and immediately felt sure that it was right for the community. Not knowing precisely where the money would come from, I offered to buy it.

During the following weeks there was a strange succession of events and discoveries. The first was that, after negotiations with bank managers and the like, I found myself able to raise the money with surprising ease. Then, although our first thought had been that another family should start the new group, I began one day to wonder if we should leave our beloved Little Gidding and move there ourselves. When I next saw Sarah I found her in tears, because she had had the same idea, and, although she hated the prospect, she was convinced it was God's will. So, with heavy hearts, we started to plan the move. Shortly afterwards I decided to research the history of the house, and found some startling connections. I found that the house was built by the Duchess of Lennox, George Herbert's patron, and that during the restoration of Leighton church parish worship was held there – so George Herbert probably held services in its parlour; that the Duchess was a Roman Catholic, and the house was used to lodge Catholic priests who came to visit Nicholas Ferrar; and, finally, that the Duchess was an ancestor of mine, my great-grandfather having married one of her descendants.

During that winter we restored and decorated the house; and, at Easter 1986, we moved there. In the course of the following year four other families and single people bought houses in the village in order to join the community. So, with remarkable speed, the new group formed, with the members walking along the village street each morning to meet for prayers in the room that George Herbert had used.

Throughout the history of Christian community the news of each new venture has tended to spread rapidly. We decided to keep publicity about ourselves to a minimum, but, as the Ferrars had found before us, people in increasing numbers wanted to come and visit. And the fame of the Ferrars themselves continues to attract thousands of pilgrims each year to the church. Like the Ferrars we wanted always to welcome guests, yet, like them, we realised that the community could easily be swamped by the demands of hospitality. We soon had to reflect carefully on how best to look after our visitors.

The majority of visitors come just for a few hours to see the church and learn something of the community. For them we provide a small exhibition room where they can see the church silver that the Ferrars made, and samples of their tapestries and book-binding; and, if they wish, they can have a cup of coffee and a cake. The guests who stay, however, present a quite different challenge. They come for a wide variety of reasons — some for a relaxing holiday within a Christian setting; others because they are searching for faith and direction in their lives; others still in order to seek personal healing. Castle House, has ample guest rooms, and also a meeting room and huts built round the garden to accommodate the groups. The guest mistress seeks to ensure that, as far as possible, the community and its members provide each guest with the care they need. As the first community found, visitors and guests are a constant source of stimulus and enjoyment.

Past and Future

We are inheritors of a vision — ordinary families meeting and praying together day by day, and supporting one another in their work and ministry — that has inspired Christians throughout the centuries. Our particular fore-bears are Nicholas Ferrar and George Herbert, whose examples and insights remain fresh and vital. They in turn were inspired by Thomas Cranmer's attempt to extend the spiritual tradition of the medieval monasteries to embrace the whole church. And monasteries them-selves were attempts to rediscover the spiritual intensity of the first Christian community in Jerusalem. When Nicholas Ferrar commended to his brother John 'the good old way', he referred not primarily to the life he had established at Little Gidding, but to a tradition of Christian communal life that goes right back to Pentecost.

But the story is never finished, and is constantly unfolding in new and unexpected ways. Until the end of human history that vision will remain alive, inspiring new communities of Christians, and re-awakening old communities. So it must be for us. We look to our history not in order to imitate those who came before, but to apply the same vision to our own circumstances. When a new person joins the community, they are called not simply to fit snugly into established patterns and routines, but also to carry the community forward by responding afresh to the age-old vision.

Our particular calling as a community is to stand between the two main traditions of Christian corporate

Castle House Leighton Bromswold

life — that of a close-knit residential group, exemplified by the monastery, in which every aspect of life is shared; and that of the parish church, with its people dispersed in a village or town, coming together only for worship. At Little Gidding the members live within a residential group, and at first glance their life may seem much like that of a monastery; but the families and single people are far more independent and self-contained than a monk or nun could be. At Leighton Bromswold and elsewhere the members live in an ordinary parish, and at first sight their communal life may seem little different to that of a normal church, but their common discipline of prayer and stewardship forges far stronger and closer bonds than can exist between ordinary church-goers. We do not for one moment imagine that our life is superior either to that of the monastery or the parish. Rather it offers a third pattern of Christian discipleship. The joy and mutual support we each derive from our member-ship of the community make us imagine that it is a way of life to which many others may be called, and we hope and pray that numerous similar communities may form in the future. Over the years we have learnt that God uses communities such as ours as witnesses to Christ, bridging the gap between the monastery and the parish. We share, in their stringent form, the high ideals of the monastery, yet as individuals and families were are no different from the kinds of people one meets in a normal parish. A close-knit Christian community, consisting of quite ordinary people, is a seed of hope in a world hungry for new vision.

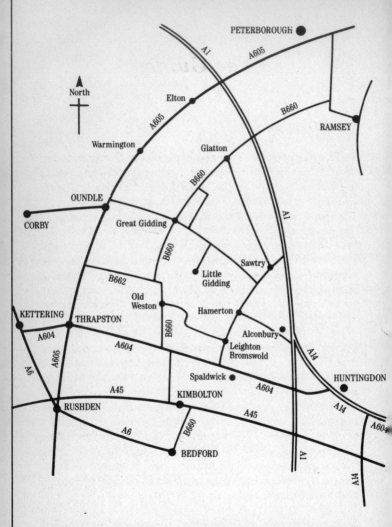

North

PETERBOROUGH

A1

A605

A605

Elton

B660

RAMSEY

Warmington

Glatton

B660

OUNDLE

A1

CORBY

Great Gidding

B660

Sawtry

B662

Little Gidding

KETTERING

Old Weston

Hamerton

Thrapston

B660

Alconbury

A604

A604

Leighton Bromswold

A6

A605

Spaldwick

A604

HUNTINGDON

A45

KIMBOLTON

A14

RUSHDEN

A45

A14

A6

B660

A1

BEDFORD

A14

A604

Please Note. This map is diagrammatic only. To get in such a large area, with such detail near the centre, it is necessary to distort distances and leave out some villages and many minor roads.

Dual carriageway ═══════

Other main roads ━━━━━━

Minor roads ──────

The Guide

Little Gidding

1 The Approach You come to Little Gidding today down a narrow lane from the north-east. On the left of the lane is the site of the old village of Gidding Parva, which died out in the Black Death of the 14th century. The humps in the field mark the old strips used by the peasants for cultivation, and, largely overgrown by brambles, there remains the old moat of the village keep. When the Ferrars bought Little Gidding in 1625 the medieval church was in ruins, the nave being used as a barn and the vestry as a pig-sty. To the east of the church was an early Tudor manor house that had fallen into decay.

2 The Exterior of the Church From the car park your first site of the church is the chancel and the east end. This is the oldest part of the present church, built in brick by the Ferrars themselves. The Ferrars restored the medieval nave, but this was largely destroyed in the Puritan raid of 1646. It was rebuilt by Nicholas Ferrar's nephew, John, in 1714. Its most distinctive feature is the west front, constructed in stone. It is unique, belonging to no architectural tradition, with a most unusual pyramid above the bellcote with three oblong openings, and a ball at the top.

3 Furnishings The interior of the church is panelled throughout. The oldest section is in the chancel, while the panelling in the nave is part of the 1714 restoration, in imitation of the earlier style. The original seating consisted of narrow benches at the base of each panel, so the congregation faced one another across a narrow aisle. In 1853 the benches were replaced by comfortable chairs. The communion table at the east end dates from the 19th century, but incorporates some of the wood from the Ferrars' table. In the Ferrars' time it would have been carried down to the middle of the chancel for a Communion service, with the congregation standing round it and the priest on the north side. On the south wall of the sanctuary, above the credence table, is a delicately carved panel which was probably part of the reredos installed by the Ferrars. Recently the original altar rails, installed by the Ferrars, have been put back; they were taken out by Hopkinson, and sold in 1884 to Prestwood Church in Bucks — which in 1988 generously returned them to Little Gidding.

4 Metalwork On the chancel step is a magnificent brass eagle lectern, made either in Flanders or in East Anglia in about 1500, and purchased by the Ferrars for the church. It stands where the Ferrars had put a pulpit, which was destroyed in the Puritan raid. Next to the lectern, attached to the panelling, is a fine wrought iron stand which in the Ferrars' time held an hour-glass for the preacher to time his sermon. On the east wall are brass tablets, which the Ferrars had made, on which are engraved the Lord's Prayer, the Ten Commandments and the Apostles' Creed. The most beautiful object dating from the Ferrars' time is the brass font – the only brass font in England — which, for security, is now exhibited in the farmhouse. Its top is in the shape of a crown, to symbolise the kingship of Christ, but it was severely battered when the Puritans threw it in the pond near the church, from which John Ferrar later retrieved it; the base is a Tudor firedog, adapted by the Ferrars for the purpose. Also in the farmhouse is the small brass crucifix from the altar, the figure on which is probably medieval. The beautiful brass candelabrum above the nave dates from the 18th century, and the delicate brass candle sconces in the chancel were made in 1920. Since there is no electricity in the church, candles are still used to light evening services.

5 Windows The glass all dates from the 1850s, and was made by the firm Ward and Hughes of London. The nave windows show the coats of arms of Charles I, Bishop John Williams, who was patron of the original community, Nicholas Ferrar, and William Hopkinson (who was responsible for the 19th century restoration). The round panes of clear glass surrounding the coats of arms were made in Italy using the same techniques as were used in medieval times. The east window shows the crucifixion, and the delicate colours are also achieved by the use of medieval techniques. The nave window openings are all original, dating from 1714, but the window in the east wall was reconstructed in the 19th century. The Ferrars had a rectangular window with stone mullions and clear glass, but Hopkinson replaced it by a larger window with a circular arch.

6 Memorials Under the path leading to the west door are buried members of the original community. Nicholas is under the table-top tomb, and his brother John lies immediately beyond him to the east. The original memorial plates have been taken from the tombs for preservation, and put on either side of the chancel arch on the inside of the church. The memorial to John Ferrar shows his coat of arms. On the back is inscribed a quotation from Psalm 37, 'Flee from evil, and do the thing that is good: and dwell for evermore'. The memorial to Nicholas's sister, Susanna, records that she bore eight sons and eight daughters — Little Gidding then, as now, was a place where children flourished.

7 Church Plate The church silver used by the Ferrars is exhibited in the farmhouse. There is a plain silver paten with no hallmark or inscription. There is also a silver flagon inscribed, 'What Sr Edwyn Sandys bequethed To The Remembrance of freindship His freind hath consecrated To The Honnour of Gods seruice, 1629', and on the handle 'for the church of Little Gidding in Huntingtonshyer'. (Sir Edwyn Sandys was an old friend of the Ferrars from Virginia Company days.) And there is a silver alms dish inscribed, 'For the Church of Little Giddin of the guift of Susan Beckwith', hallmarked for 1634. (Susan Beckwith's son had lived with the Ferrars for a year in 1632–3 as part of his education, and the alms dish is a token of gratitude.)

8 King's Close The field to the west of the church, known as King's Close, is the site of the original community. The manor house stood abut 50 yards from the church, on land artificially levelled; the house burnt down in the early 19th century. Beyond it was a fine avenue of trees leading down to the Alconbury Brook. This was the original approach to Little Gidding and was named King's Close after King Charles's visit in 1642. To one side of the avenue was an orchard in which the women of the community strolled on Sunday afternoons.

9 Community Buildings The farmhouse, now the centre of the present community, was built by William Hopkinson in the 1840s. It does, however, incorporate in its interior walls some Tudor brickwork from one wing of the original manor house; and the community chapel has across its ceiling two old, charred beams which were probably rescued from the burnt remains of the old house. The main residential buildings of the community are round the old farmyard to the west of the farmhouse. At the entrance are the charming pigsties, now used as sheds, which T. S. Eliot mentions in his poem 'Little Gidding'. The block of four houses along the far side of the yard was built in 1980 using old materials, and incorporating the timber frame of a barn which the Ferrars built. To their right is a 19th century brick barn and the old workshops, converted into further accommodation for members. To either side of the farm-yard is a large workshop and a farm building put up by the community in the mid-1980s, and beyond them is six acres of land cultivated by the community.

Leighton Bromswold

1 The Approach Leighton Bromswold is about five miles south of Little Gidding. As you approach from Hamerton the magnificent square church tower is visible from two or three miles away, standing on a prominent ridge. To the south-east of the church you can see, through the trees, Castle House built in deep red Jacobean brick. On the other side of the church is the fine avenue of lime trees laid out by the Cliftons, along which the village is built. In Saxon times this was the centre of the Leightonstone Hundred, and the stone seat of judgement can be seen just outside the church gate.

2 The Exterior of the Church The tower is a remarkable example of English classical architecture. It was built in 1634, in honour of George Herbert who had died a year earlier, and is thus at the beginning of the period when English architects like Inigo Jones were seeking to reproduce precisely the Italian architecture of Palladio. Its form is that of a medieval church tower, but its rounded arches and square windows, and the obelisks at the top, are classical. The south door of the church, dating from the 13th century, is the finest part of the medieval church still in tact, with its delicate carved arch mouldings. Continuing round the church on the outside there are magnificent rainwater heads and down-pipes, also dating from 1634, one of which on the chancel wall shows the crests of the Herberts and the Cliftons.

3 Woodwork The interior woodwork and furnishing of the church dates almost entirely to George Herbert's restoration, and is the finest example of early 17th century church furnishings in the country. When George Herbert took charge of the church, the roof had collapsed and had to be entirely rebuilt. Thus, standing now in the middle of the nave and looking up, one sees the sturdy joinery of 17th century craftsmen. On either side of the chancel arch are what appear to be two identical pulpits with large sounding-boards above. The right-hand one is, in fact, the priest's desk from which he leads prayers, and the left-hand one, the pulpit – George Herbert wanted to symbolize the equal importance of preaching and prayer by putting the pulpit and stall at the same height. George Herbert also put in the pews throughout the church, and the layout of the pews in the chancel is quite remarkable. They are not choir stalls, as we might imagine, but seats for the celebration of communion — the communion table would have been brought down into the middle of the chancel, and at the offertory the congregation would have come up from the nave to sit in the chancel.

4 Windows The windows in the transepts date mostly from the late 14th century, but those in the chancel offer an intriguing puzzle to the historian. The chancel is beautifully light, surrounded by large windows with clear glass which are in the medieval style. However, closer investigation shows that the side windows are too tall for the roof line of the church in the 13th century. Thus what appears to have happened is that in the 15th century the chancel roof was raised, and the first windows on either side of the chancel were put in. The other windows all date from George Herbert's restoration in the 17th century, but recall an earlier style. The four side windows with their Y-tracery are of 13th century style, while the east window is a simplified version of the style of two centuries later. Thus we can see that George Herbert was keen to preserve the medieval atmosphere of the church, while at the same time adapting the interior layout to suit the 17th century pattern of worship.

5 Castle House Castle House was originally a gate-house, built in 1616, but the large mansion that was planned for the field behind it was never constructed. The architect was John Thorpe, the leading draftsman of his day, but as soon as the gatehouse was complete Sir Gervaise Clifton, the Lord of the Manor, was imprisoned in the Tower of London where he died. His daughter Katherine, who married the Duke of Lennox, never lived there, but converted it into a hunting lodge. She filled in the arch to make a central room (leaving the old hinge-brackets still visible), and built a wing onto the south-west — it was this wing that George Herbert used for parish worship when the church was being restored. At both the front and the back are two Tuscan columns; above the front ones are short pilasters with an unusual pattern of little pyramids, and at the top a balustrade. These decorations are splendid examples of the rather eccentric classical style brought over by Flemish stonemasons in the early 17th century. They are playful impressions rather than precise copies of the classical architecture of Palladio in Italy. The house was altered at the end of the 19th century, when an entrance hall was constructed between the two front towers, and Jacobean fireplaces and a staircase taken from Stow Longa manor, which was being demolished, were installed.